A PICTORIAL HISTORY OF
JOSEPH
STALIN

NIGEL BLUNDELL

JG PRESS

Published in the United States of America 1996 by JG Press
Distributed by World Publications, Inc.

The JG Press is a trademark of
JG Press, Inc.
455 Somerset Avenue
North Dighton, MA 02764

ISBN 1-57215-138-2

Picture Acknowledgements
All the photographs in this book were supplied by the
Society for Co-operation in Russian and Soviet Studies,
320, Brixton Road,
London, SW9 6AB
England.

This edition produced 1996 by the
Promotional Reprint Company Ltd
Deacon House, 65 Old Church Street
Chelsea, London SW3 5BS

Publishing Manager *Casey Horton*
Design Manager *Ming Cheung*
Editor *Paul Brewer*
Designer *Sunita Gahir*

Printed and bound in Hong Kong

19.95

CONTENTS

INTRODUCTION

HE was the son of a serf yet managed to claw his way to power over the heads of intellectuals, politicians and statesmen.

He espoused great ideals yet he was a streetfighting, boorish bully.

He championed the cause of the masses yet delivered them into mass graves.

He was heralded as a great general yet his ineptitude lost him entire armies.

This astonishingly paradoxical figure was Joseph Stalin, tyrant of the vast Soviet Union, then the largest state on Earth. Stalin, which means 'Man of Steel', was a name he adopted at the age of 34. A better title for him might have been 'Man of Blood'.

For apart from being a war leader who sacrificed his own forces in millions, he was arguably the most destructive human being of the 20th century.

Adolf Hitler is normally considered the world's worst mass murderer. But although millions died at Hitler's behest, Stalin was responsible for even more senseless deaths. At least eight million people were killed while this granite-faced dictator ruled the Soviet Union. Millions more died as a direct result of his ideologically inspired policies.

Left: This caricature of Stalin, perhaps superficially humanising, retains a hint of some innate malevolence in the man. The dog's glaring eye and Stalin's raised eyebrow seem full of threat.

Opposite right: The 'Man of Steel', the 'dear Leader and Teacher', the Hero of the Soviet Union – the message of this officially approved portrait is loud and clear.

His motives were confused: a deadly brew of revenge, ambition, fear and bloodlust.

Stalin liked to watch the interrogation of political suspects by his secret police and ordered them to 'beat, beat and beat again until they come crawling to you on their bellies with confessions in their teeth.'

These words were uttered by an international statesman and world leader who sat with giants such as Churchill and Roosevelt and who single-handedly changed the course of history for dangerous decades.

The man who forged the Iron Curtain, whose personality cult attained Pharaonic proportions, was only in death revealed to – and reviled by – his people as an idol with feet of clay.

ORIGINS OF A TYRANT

JOSEPH Stalin, as we now know him, was born on 21 December 1879, the darkest day of the year. The lusty cries of the newly-born infant told his mother Ekaterina all she need to know: that he was a strong, healthy child, perfect except that the second and third toes of his left foot were joined together. With his safe arrival in the world, her dearest wishes came true. This was her fourth pregnancy yet none of the other babies had lived. She resolved that Iosif Vissarionovich Dzhugashvili would be a priest by way of thanks to God.

Home was little more than a shack in Gori, a small town in Georgia, a country then a part of the Russian Empire in the Caucusus mountains bordering on Turkey. There was one room only and the few sticks of furniture in it were simply crafted out of wood. Stalin's hovel still exists today, dwarfed by a marble mock-temple built to honour the birthplace during his era in power.

LEFT: The house in Gori, Georgia, where Stalin was born in the small flat of the shoemaker Vissarion Dzhugashvili.

RIGHT: The youthful Stalin is captured in this police photograph taken about 1900.

LEFT: Stalin's mother, Ekaterina Geladze, wife of Vissarion Dzhugashvili, was a pious woman who was desperate for her son to escape a life in poverty.

RIGHT: Between March 1914 and the end of 1916 Stalin was exiled to the Siberian village of Kureika.

Ekaterina, or Keke as she was better known, was determined that her adored only son would escape the grinding poverty she had known all her life. To this end, she slaved as a washerwoman and at other menial labours, saving enough money to buy him an education. She was poor and illiterate but even she could see that this was the only possible means of liberation from a dire existence.

Her fondness of little Iosif (or Joseph), who was nicknamed Soso, was beyond question. Her boundless motherly love didn't prevent her from meting out beatings to her mischievous son. However, the swipes he suffered from her were nothing compared to the beatings he endured from his father.

Vissarion Dzhugashvili inflicted vicious punishment on his only son, much of it apparently carried out for the sheer pleasure it gave him. Vissarion was a cobbler but he sacrificed his skills for the sake of hard drinking. In addition to the brutal beatings he took himself, the young Stalin witnessed his loutish father attack his beloved mother. Yet Keke was no wilting flower. Although slight and pale, she lashed out at her errant husband many times while they lived together. It was during one such bout of violence between the couple that an outraged Stalin grabbed a kitchen knife and hurled it at Vissarion. Stalin instantly ran off and sought refuge from his father's wrath with a neighbour, an act which probably saved his skin.

When times got hard, Vissarion took a job in a boot factory away from home, although he returned periodically to terrorise his wife and son. When he died in a drunken brawl in 1890, he was something of a tramp. His passing was nothing short of a blessed relief for Stalin.

If poverty and abuse were not enough to contend with, Stalin experienced other disadvantages in childhood. An attack of smallpox which almost killed him left him severely pockmarked. The scars were so deep that photographs taken of him much later were doctored to disguise the disfigurement. In addition, his left arm was shorter than his right by several inches, possibly due to an accident in which he was run over by a carriage while watching a religious festival.

Stalin was not going to let any of this stand in his way, however. The traumas of childhood did not make him withdrawn, as is often the case. When he began school in September 1888, rather than being bullied, Stalin was himself the aggressor.

LEFT: In 1898, Iosif Dzhugashvili took the pseudonym 'Koba' and began leading a Marxist study circle among railway workers that met in this Tbilisi house.

RIGHT: In 1935 Lavrenti Beria, then boss of the Georgian Communist Party, constructed a marble edifice over the birthplace of Stalin.

Schoolmates have testified that the young Stalin was awestruck by the wild and spectacular terrain of Georgia, although he had no particular respect for the wildlife within it. He frequently passed the time by hurling stones at birds. He loved books, especially adventure stories, and read many which were banned in the classroom. Revealing still more of an artistic nature, Stalin loved to sketch. Also, he sang beautifully in melodic tenor tones. Many of these qualities he suppressed long before he reached power for fear others would regard them as weaknesses or indulgences.

Following his six-year spell at the Gori church school, Stalin headed for the seminary training his mother always vowed he would have. In 1894 he went to the theological seminary at Tbilisi, a major centre some 70 km/45 miles southeast of his home town. He was a boarder, which meant that he was exposed to the harsh regime of the seminary round the clock.

The studies were demanding and Stalin acquired a working knowledge of classical languages as well as Orthodox church theology. He also devoured a whole range of books on subjects banned by the seminary – often getting himself into trouble in the process. Stalin was by now schooled far beyond the dreams of most Georgian boys.

It was while he was preparing for the priesthood in this repressive environment that Stalin got his first taste for the politics of change. Seminaries, top-heavy with regulations and renowned for the cruelty of their masters, were paradoxically popular breeding grounds for revolutionaries. Secret meetings were held to discuss Marxist theory and to debate the need for revolution.

By 1898 Stalin was a member of a local Georgian Marxist organisation called *Mesame Dasi* or Group Three. His behaviour worsened at the seminary. He refused to work and was rude to the monks who tried to teach him. The following year, he left the seminary; if he was not expelled, he most certainly departed under a cloud. It was a move his mother regretted for the rest of her days – even when her son held sway over the entire Russian Empire.

THE SICK MAN OF EUROPE

BY the turn of the century Russia was on the verge of revolutionary turmoil. Terrorist assassination of high-ranking civil servants was chronic. Trades unions – some organised by police spies – in spite of being legally banned were demanding better pay and conditions for the country's extremely impoverished industrial workers. The peasants had experienced a famine in 1897. There was no parliament in which grievances could be vented. The secret police, the Okhrana, were able to make arbitrary arrests and imprison people without a trial. The country's new tsar, Nicholas II, had come to the throne in 1894. He confessed to his future brother-in-law Grand Duke Alexander: 'I am not prepared to be a tsar. I never wanted to be one. I know nothing of the business of ruling.'

Tsar Nicholas was married to a German princess, Alexandra of Hesse-Darmstadt, a grandchild of Britain's Queen Victoria. Although worshipped by her husband, this handsome, imperious woman was an unpopular figure. Within the walls of their palaces, however, the couple were idyllically happy. They had

LEFT: 'Alms' – a posed photograph by the Russian A Karelin captures the vast gulf of wealth between bourgeois Russians and their poor compatriots.

RIGHT: *On the Barricades*, a painting by Roman Yakovlev, commemorates the 1905 revolution in Moscow, in which vicious streetfighting occurred.

four daughters and then, in 1904, Alexei. Their joy at the birth of a male heir to the Russian throne soon turned to dismay when they realised he suffered from haemophilia. The condition, inherent in the royal families of Europe, was a disabling one. Every bump or scratch would gush with blood and even the most experienced medic had difficulty in stemming the flow. The tsar and his tsarina focused their energies on the survival of their only son, at the expense of the survival of the Russian Empire.

The writing was on the wall long before the revolution of 1917. On 9 January 1905 aggrieved St Petersburg factory workers marched to the Winter Palace to present a petition to the Tsar, whom they thought of as their 'Little Father'. They were led by Father George Gapon, a trade union activist priest who was on the police payroll. The tsar's officials refused to recognise that the demonstrators' pitiful wages and appalling living conditions fuelled a burning desire for change. Their reply was an order to the army to open fire – and 500 men, women and children were killed, in an incident branded 'Bloody Sunday'.

A further 200 people were killed in April 1912 when soldiers opened fire on 5000 men, women and children striking at the Lena goldfield in Siberia in protest at their starvation wages. Strikes and subversion became commonplace. In repressing these political gestures, the army and the Okhrana showed a blatant disregard for human rights or life.

It was this combination which transformed peaceable Russian workers into hard-bitten revolutionaries. Russia's economy was being catapulted headlong into the industrial age, as its vast storehouse of natural resources were put to productive use. The mines of Siberia, the oil fields of Azerbaijan and the fertile farmland of the steppes gave the empire a leg-up into the industrialised world. Yet the profits went into but few pockets. Those who toiled underground in the mines or braved the smog of the smoking oil wells were still hungry and clad in rags.

Against this grim background came the First World War (1914-18), with ill-equipped Russian soldiers pitted against Germany's well-oiled war machine. The result was predictable. Whole armies of Russians were slaughtered or taken prisoner. Peasants were rounded up in the Russian countryside to take the place of the fallen at the front lines. As the losses mounted, so did the bitterness of the working people, who knew full well that they were only being used as cannon fodder.

By September 1915, Tsar Nicholas was concerned enough about the failures of his army in battle to leave the palace and head for the front line to command the troops personally. His actions were well-intentioned

LEFT: The 1905 revolution spread throughout the country. This demonstration took place in Kiev, in the Ukraine.

RIGHT: Father Gapon, shown here with the tsar's chief of police, General I A Fullon, led the workers' march that culminated in 'Bloody Sunday'.

Conditions for workers in tsarist Russia were the most primitive in the industrial countries of Europe. Miners (left) and blast-furnace workers (right) were members of a workforce suffering low wages for long hours without any form of legal trade unions to defend their rights.

but entirely foolhardy. The catastrophes of the battlefield were soon held to be his personal responsibility.

At home, meanwhile, Alexandra had fallen under the spell of a grubby, lecherous monk named Rasputin. The tsarina appeared little more than a puppet to the conniving monk, whom she took to her heart because of his apparent power to heal the sickly Tsarevich Alexei. Rasputin had an army of supporters, all believing that he was gifted. Others thought him a malevolent force who was making the royal couple look like idiots. On 29 December 1916 a group of noblemen took matters into their own hands by poisoning, shooting and then battering the raging Rasputin, who refused to die. When they finally disposed of his body in a freezing river, it is thought he was still alive. But the damage had been done. The authority of Russia's royal rulers had been shattered, and it was only months before the tsarist regime was toppled for good.

Stalin, after leaving the Tbilisi seminary, channelled all his energies towards the coming revolution. From the turn of the century, the revolutionary movement had spread its tentacles across the empire. Stalin concentrated his efforts in Georgia.

In December 1899 he found a job as a clerk at the Tbilisi Physical Institute. He enjoyed free lodgings and a wage of 20 roubles a month. This is perhaps the only employment Stalin held down in his life. And his time in the post was short-lived. In May 1901 the police had raided his lodgings in a crackdown on subversives. Although Stalin escaped arrest, he deemed it impossible to return to his workplace. He thought it only a matter of time before he would be incarcerated like so many of his contemporaries. His only choice to avoid detention was to go underground.

Now he lived life as a rebel on a police 'wanted' list. He was one of a number who passed their days writing and printing revolutionary newspapers and pamphlets. By night there were meetings, some stormy and uproarious, all held in secret. He and others would graduate to robbery and thuggery to find more money for the movement during the years before the 1917 revolution.

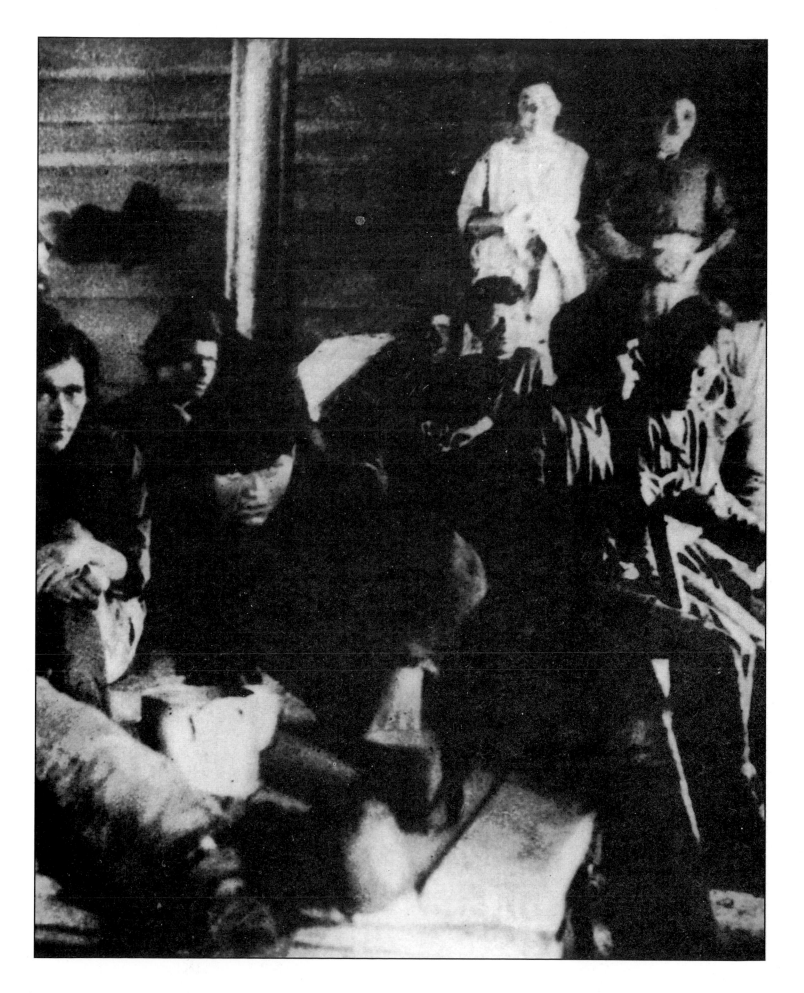

The shadowy figure of the agitator Stalin was behind a May Day march in Tbilisi in 1901 during which 14 people were wounded and more than 50 arrested. Once again, Stalin slipped through the clutches of the police and soldiers who went into action that day. On 9 March 1902, Stalin helped lead a demonstration at Batumi. This time the troops opened fire, killing 15 and injuring 54 more.

By now Stalin was a member of a revolutionary committee. He believed wholeheartedly in the extremes of the revolution. He was not popular, plaguing his fellow members with his arrogant brand of badgering. Anyone with views which differed, if only slightly, to his own, he would dismiss rudely, with ferocious hectoring. The meetings must have been noisy ones. The militants in the movement, the Bolsheviks, were beginning a bitter divorce from the moderates, the Mensheviks.

The secret police finally caught up with Stalin in April 1902. He was held until July 1903, when he was exiled without trial to Siberia, thousands of miles from his home. Within seven months he escaped, with apparent ease, to continue his illicit activities.

Speculation has been rife that Stalin was in fact a spy for the secret police during this time. Certainly his good fortune at slipping through the fingers of the police time and again seemed to some to be more than just luck. Others even doubted that he was sent to Siberia at all. After all, if he was not in the pay of the police, how was he supporting himself without work?

There have been many vain attempts to prove that self-seeker Stalin was in those days a traitor to his cause. But there is little doubt that Stalin did betray an Armenian Bolshevik, Stepan Shaumyan, to the police in 1905. Shaumyan did not favour the heavy-handed, violent tactics advocated by Stalin. His reasoned arguments swayed many, and the rivalry between him and Stalin escalated – until Shaumyan was suddenly arrested at his secret hideaway. It was an address known only to Stalin.

Stalin was only a bit-part player during the unrest of 1905 – the year of the Potemkin mutiny, the establishment of workers' soviets (councils) in St Petersburg and Moscow, and the bloody suppression of the latter. At the end of that year, he attended a conference in Finland and met the man whose influential writing had become his sacred texts: Vladimir Ilich Lenin.

His first impressions of the revolutionary master were contradictory. Here was the man to whom everybody deferred, yet he displayed none of the pomposity, posturing or obvious fervour that were the trademarks of his ilk. Lenin cut a distinctively unimpressive figure, plainly clad and quietly spoken. Stalin

Left: Russian field guns shell German positions during the First World War. The failures of the Russian armed forces in this conflict and the Russo-Japanese war of 1904-5 helped create a revolutionary situation.

Right: During the 1905 revolution, Stalin played a comparatively inconspicuous role, although he did address a number of mass meetings, captured in this painting by Abegyana.

LEFT: Alexandra Kollontai was one of the Old Bolsheviks (members of Lenin's party before 1917). She was to survive almost all her male counterparts, and was Soviet ambassador to Sweden for many years.

RIGHT: The Bolshevik movement was very much a personal faction of Lenin's within the Russian Social Democratic Workers' party. Lenin's genius was to perceive exactly the right balance between theory and action in order to accomplish political success.

was at first bemused by this modesty: 'I had hoped to see the mountain eagle of our party, the great man, great physically as well as politically... How great was my disappointment to see a most ordinary-looking man.' Stalin, however, quickly realised that the mere presence of Lenin was enough to make people sit up and listen. It was lesson in understatement that Stalin put to good use in later life – and was all the more menacing because of it. Lenin viewed Stalin as a loyal, talented Bolshevik worth watching. The Bolshevik leader encouraged Stalin to produce a theoretical work on nationalism and Marxism in 1912.

Stalin was temporarily exiled once more on 29 September 1908 following his arrest in March of that year. No doubt rankled by the insolent, cocky young man, police seized him once again on 23 March 1910. There followed spells in jail and months of freedom, in which Stalin played a cat-and-mouse game with the authorities. The internment gave him a new political dignity and authority, and he was promoted within the revolutionary movement from his Georgian realm to centre stage at St Petersburg.

The end of his many periods of exile came in 1916 when he was told to leave his assigned home near the Arctic Circle to be assessed for military service. His disabled arm meant he was no good for soldiering. But now the country was on the brink of revolution.

POLITICS OF POWER

WITH the overthrow of the tsarist regime in March 1917 came a breath of fresh air for Russians. Under the liberal, reforming Provisional Government, they could at last consort with whomever they pleased, pronounce their opinions freely and read the newspaper of their choice. Never before in their history had the people been free from the repression. After the October Revolution and the civil war that followed, when the Bolsheviks took charge, it would be years before they were free again.

Predictably, there was chaos immediately following the overthrow of the imperial Establishment. Age-old systems of policing and government were dismantled but there was nothing to put in their place. The Provisional Government flailed helplessly in the face of national disarray. It persevered with an unpopular war the country was losing. Civil unrest escalated. Among the agitators were the Bolsheviks, including Joseph Stalin.

With a membership of some 40,000, the Bolshevik faction was ready and willing to take power. In Petrograd (formerly St Petersburg) they dominated the deliberations of the local Soviet – a council of workers' and soldiers' deputies. When Lenin arrived in Russia from his exile in Finland in October, he declared: 'History will not forgive us if we do not take power now.' His order for revolution finally came, scrawled in a child's notebook. The date was 25 October by the outdated Julian calendar then used in Russia, or 7 November by the Gregorian calendar prevalent in the rest of Europe.

BELOW LEFT: A demonstration in the streets of Moscow during the March 1917 revolution that overthrew the tsarist autocracy.

RIGHT: During the summer of 1917, opposition to the war policy of the Provisional Government that succeeded the tsarist regime led to protests in cities across Russia. This one took place in Moscow's Theatre Square.

BELOW: Demonstrators out in force in Petrograd during the July days of 1917. At this time, hotheads in the Bolshevik Military Organisation attempted to topple the government. As a result, Lenin and Trotsky were forced temporarily into hiding.

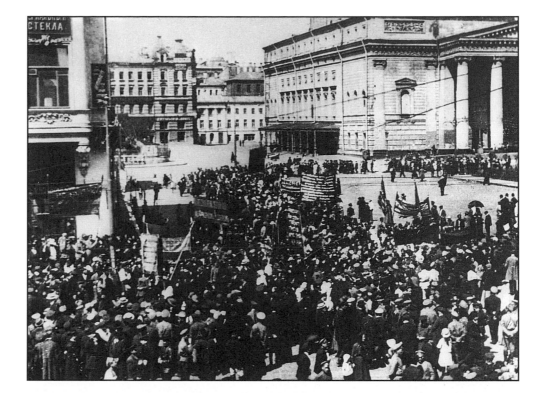

LEFT: A Stalinist view of the October Revolution – Lenin and Stalin jointly plotting the downfall of the Provisional Government. In truth, Stalin's position in the Bolshevik leadership left him a spectator while Lenin and Trotsky organised the coup.

RIGHT: The backbone of the Petrograd Soviet's military force were Red Guards such as these men from the Putilove plant.

Such key communication points as railway stations and telephone exchanges were occupied by Bolshevik troops in the early hours. By dawn the national bank was under siege, as was the Winter Palace, the seat of the Provisional Government. There were comparatively few deaths in the Red coup, and it was not unpopular. The Bolsheviks and their left-wing allies wanted an end to the war. There was hope of salvation for the people of Russia when the Brest-Litovsk Treaty, was signed in March 1918. The Russian Empire was dismembered by the treaty, with the Ukraine, Finland, Poland and the Baltic States given their liberty, and part of Belorussia ceded to Germany. However, there was no end in sight to the bloodshed.

Armed forces loyal to the Tsar – known as 'Whites'– were still in the field. Foreign soldiers, including British, American, Japanese and French, arrived to back the 'Whites'. There were also troops who still supported the Provisional Government. In addition, there were resident foreign workers and prisoners of war, including 40,000 Czechs eager to return home and prepared to fight if necessary, not to mention a potent force of anarchists who would take on all-comers. It was a combustible cocktail. The minority-supported Bolshevik revolutionary government could easily have been destabilised.

But Lenin's way out was to rule with an iron fist. His defence minister, Leon Trotsky, wielded fierce discipline to build and control an army of some 5 million. He used the death penalty liberally and, when troops had been disloyal, ordered that every tenth man should be shot.

The imperial family remained captives in the Urals town of Ekaterinburg until 16 July 1918. On that day local Bolsheviks, nervous that the family could be used as a damaging rallying point for loyalists, shot the Tsar, his wife, their five children and their servants. This kind of brutality became a hallmark of the

ABOVE: Lenin's draft of the proclamation of Soviet power was written in a child's notebook.

FAR RIGHT: The cruiser *Aurora* shelled Petrograd's Winter Palace, the seat of the Provisional Government, during the assault by Red Guards.

RIGHT: The Decree of Soviet Power issued on 25 October 1917 (old style) marked the foundation of the Soviet Union. This social experiment on a massive scale was to last a little more than 74 years.

От Военно-Революціоннаго Комитета при Петроградскомъ Совѣтѣ Рабочихъ и Солдатскихъ Депутатовъ.

Къ Гражданамъ Россіи.

Временное Правительство низложено. Государственная власть перешла въ руки органа Петроградскаго Совѣта Рабочихъ и Солдатскихъ Депутатовъ Военно-Революціоннаго Комитета, стоящаго во главѣ Петроградскаго пролетаріата и гарнизона.

Дѣло, за которое боролся народъ: немедленное предложеніе демократическаго мира, отмѣна помѣщичьей собственности на землю, рабочій контроль надъ производствомъ, созданіе Совѣтскаго Правительства — это дѣло обезпечено.

ДА ЗДРАВСТВУЕТЪ РЕВОЛЮЦІЯ РАБОЧИХЪ, СОЛДАТЪ И КРЕСТЬЯНЪ!

Военно-Революціонный Комитетъ
при Петроградскомъ Совѣтѣ
Рабочихъ и Солдатскихъ Депутатовъ.

25 октября 1917 г. 10 ч. утра.

Bolshevik regime, although the atrocities of the civil war were by no means the preserve of the Reds alone: the Whites were equally guilty of inhuman outrages during the civil war.

Stalin revelled in the burgeoning power of the Bolsheviks. He became intoxicated by the expanding bureaucracy which was establishing itself. Officially, his role was as People's Commissar for Nationalities, but his brief was far broader. He began by travelling the country to mobilise support. On 6 June 1918 he found himself in the city of Tsaritsyn with a force of Red Guards and two armoured trains. Under the guise of 'director-general of food supplies' in south Russia, he began building his own empire, demanding soldiers and supplies from Moscow. In return he supplied food for the capital.

Stalin even became a kind of local warlord, launching military operations against the Whites. He achieved considerable successes, and the city that held his headquarters was later named after him: Stalingrad. The conqueror returned a hero, to take his place beside Lenin. It was early days but Stalin could clearly see a route to power.

With other trusted aides travelling the country, Lenin found himself ever more dependent on Stalin, who became responsible for signing key orders. Stalin was something of a troubleshooter. All impudence and brawn, he thought nothing of issuing the most ruthless diktats to advance Lenin's cause. Stalin was flexible and responsive and achieved results. He made it his business to know everybody who mattered – and

LEFT: A still taken from Eisenstein's film *October* shows the storming of the Winter Palace. The real event was perhaps not quite visibly as dramatic as this, but was certainly a historical landmark of the highest order.

RIGHT: Yakov Sverdlov, probably the one Old Bolshevik who could have withstood the rise of Stalin, died of the Spanish flu in 1919.

everything they did. His nickname was 'Comrade Card-Index'. Soon Lenin found it difficult to operate effectively without him.

Lenin's health never really recovered from an attempt on his life made by a pistol-toting social democrat, Fanya Dora-Kaplan, in August 1918. Four years later he suffered a series of strokes, the last of which killed him on 21 January 1924. Stalin was poised to take his place. Lenin, however, was not completely beguiled by Stalin. He had fallen out with him shortly before his death, when Stalin had rudely treated Lenin's wife, Nadezhda Krupskaia, over a small matter, as the words of his last testament reveal:

Stalin is too rude and this fault, quite tolerable in our midst or in relations among Communists, becomes intolerable for one who holds the office of General Secretary. Therefore I propose to the comrades that they consider a means of removing Stalin from the post and appointing to it another person…more patient, more loyal, more polite and more considerate to comrades, less capricious and so forth.

Graciously, Stalin offered to resign but his comrades refused to allow it. Without realising it, they were offering the path to power to Stalin the human steamroller, and he would flatten any obstacle along the way.

After Lenin's death Stalin was part of a trio who controlled a majority on the Central Committee. The other two were Grigory Zinoviev, the Leningrad party boss, and Lev Kamenev, Zinoviev's long-standing ally in the party. Trotsky's supporters were in a minority, but Stalin knew that from him came the greatest

BELOW LEFT: German soldiers unload grain during the occupation of the Ukraine after the signing of the Brest-Litovsk treaty in March 1918.

RIGHT: These pro-tsarist demonstators were part of the substantial minority who were prepared to take up arms against the revolutionary regime to restore the tsarist autocracy.

BELOW: A well-equipped Red Army company poses for the camera. The Bolshevik regime built its armed forces from a demoralised, defeated tsarist army and untrained workers' militia.

threat to his position. Trotsky was closely identified with Lenin's revolution. As war commissar between 1918 and 1920, he had proved himself through the creation of the Red Army and its ensuing successes. And he was far from impressed by Stalin, calling him 'the most outstanding mediocrity in our party'.

Yet Trotsky's political position was weak. During the revolution he had come into conflict with both Stalin and Zinoviev and their mutual antagonisms had continued into the 1920s. Furthermore, Trotsky's own philosophy – 'My party, right or wrong.' – prevented him making a bid for power without the support of a majority of Communists.

When battle was joined after Lenin's death it was over the future direction of the Soviet Union as a socialist state. Stalin took the unorthodox Marxist position that a proletarian revolution was possible in a comparatively backward country – Lenin's theory of the weakest link. Externally, he was concerned with fending off possible anti-Bolshevik interventions by capitalist countries. Internally, his aim was to drag ramshackle Russia into the modern age – no matter what the cost in terms of human misery. His policy was: 'Socialism in one country.' Trotsky, on the other hand, believed the Soviet Union would founder unless revolutions occurred in the 'advanced capitalist' countries of Western Europe. The crux of his thinking was that working classes everywhere should accelerate the drive to overthrow the common enemy, capitalism.

For a while, Trotsky was prepared to keep his own counsel to avoid a split in the party. But Stalin knew that, as a rival, the fervent international revolutionary would remain a thorn in his side. The ground on which their battle was fought was economic policy. Trotsky and his followers supported the rapid

LEFT: Stalin, shown here in Red Army uniform, had a Civil War record of insubordination leading to repeated failures.

TOP RIGHT: Stalin urges the men of the 1st Cavalry Army into battle in 1919.

BOTTOM RIGHT: Agit-train 'Red Caucasus' was part of a national campaign to raise the political awareness of the Soviet peoples during the early 1920s.

industrialisation of the Soviet Union and the forced collectivisation of the peasants. At this time, Stalin sided with another leading Old Bolshevik, Nikolai Bukharin, in maintaining the so-called New Economic Policy, which favoured gradual industrialisation and paying a market price for farm produce to independent smallholders. In July 1926, following a long struggle over the direction of economic policy, Trotsky lost his seat in the Politburo. In November 1927, he was expelled from the party. In 1929, Stalin banished Trotsky from the Soviet Union for ever.

It was not enough. From his places of exile, Trotsky waged a war of words against his old rival, accusing him of deviating from Leninist principles, and continued to contact potential anti-Stalin members of the

TOP RIGHT: Even as late as 1925 Soviet farmers were using medieval methods.

LEFT: A student in an adult literacy class shows how much he has learned. The Communist regime put great emphasis on educating people whom the tsarist autocracy had been content to leave ignorant.

BOTTOM RIGHT: New tractors delivered in 1925 were part of the drive to mechanise Soviet agriculture and increase its productivity.

Left: Lenin's wife, Nadezhda Krupskaya, had little love for Stalin, whom she considered an ill-mannered bully.

Top Right: Lenin, holidaying in early August 1922, had little more than five months before he experienced his first stroke.

Bottom Right: In 1922 strains began to appear in the political relationship between Stalin and Lenin. There are plenty of signs that the revolutionary mastermind planned to take the Georgian general secretary down a peg or two.

party in the hope of forming an oppositionist bloc. An outraged Stalin heaped condemnation on Trotsky, holding him and his machinations responsible for any disasters that befell the Soviet state. In 1936, following the first show trial at which Trotsky was a defendant in absentia, a warrant was issued for his arrest. The matter was put in the hands of his secret police, the NKVD (the Russian acronym for People's Commissariat for Internal Affairs), Trotsky's fate was sealed.

In 1937 Trotsky settled in Mexico. Here, on 20 August 1940, Frank Jacson, supposedly a Belgian mountaineer and writer, smashed an ice axe into Trotsky's head. Trotsky died 26 hours later in hospital. His assassin, hand-picked by the NKVD, was in reality a Spanish Communist called Ramòn Mercador. The authority of Josef Stalin as leader of the Communist movement was now unrivalled.

FIVE YEAR PLANS

STALIN had ambitions for the Soviet Union. He longed to see his country at the top of the international industrial league. He wrote: 'We are 50 or a 100 years behind the advanced countries. We must make good this distance in 10 years. Either we do it or we will be crushed.' He was prepared to pay any price for the privilege of saving his nation. And the cost came in terms of human lives. For the path that Stalin followed in his quest led to the deaths of untold millions. People died of exhaustion, cold and starvation. In the name of Communism, Stalin exhibited the worst excesses of capitalism. As he did so, his people lived miserable existences in order to pursue the unattainable goals he had set them.

Grand plans for industrial centres were drawn up. The first Five Year Plan was carried out between 1928 and 1932 with some success. People worked hard with a will to attain the goal of a prosperous Soviet state. One Ukrainian miner, Alexei Stakhanov, cut out 102 tons of coal in one shift instead of the usual seven. He was heralded as a hero of the revolution.

LEFT: The new city of Magnitogorsk in the southern Urals was built in the wilderness. These men helped construct the metallurgical plant, one of the greatest accomplishments of the Five Year Plan.

ABOVE RIGHT: Stalin with henchmen Lazar Kaganovich (right) and Sergo Ordzhonikidze (background) inspect a new model caterpillar tractor in 1935.

But it was impossible to maintain this level of production across the board for long, and the rewards presented to workers were few. Conditions were grim, strikes banned and, in a climate of industrial repression, workers flitted from job to job. A worker in the coal and iron ore industries in 1930 stayed in a job for an average of just four months. When targets were not met, Stalin declared that there were wreckers or saboteurs at work and show trials were held to root them out.

Nevertheless, the lure of employment in industry still drew thousands of peasants from the country to the town. Accordingly, there were fewer people producing food. Those that were producing grain were belligerent because, they claimed, the price offered by the government was too low. By 1928 the production of food was so low that the towns, with their freshly boosted populations, began to starve. So did the men

LEFT: Stalin sits with Soviet head of state Mikhail Kalinin (far left) and Lazar Kaganovich (centre), during a congress of collective farm workers.

RIGHT: The First Five Year Plan (1928-33) saw a tremendous shift of people from villages in the countryside to cities old and new. These workers from Belorussia are on their way east to the massive industrial development of the Kuzbass in western Siberia.

of the Red Army. Stalin knew that danger loomed if discontent spread within the ranks of the powerful armed forces. He decided upon action.

In speeches, Stalin made mention of the threat of war and the need to strengthen the Soviet state for the coming conflict. Looking back, there was scant evidence for this view, which was little more than an illusion wrought by Stalin to rally the people. It worked, for a brutal era got underway with barely a peep of objection from the masses.

He could have put the price of grain up. That would have stimulated its supply, but made it more expensive for those living in cities and towns, who – according to Marxist theory – were the backbone of the proletarian state. Suspicions that the peasants were withholding grain as part of an organised opposition to socialism festered in Stalin's mind. His answer was to collectivise agriculture. Collectivisation meant state ownership of the land and its crops. Hand in hand came agriculture's mechanisation.

To inspire support for this radical measure, he focused the blame for his country's hard times on the 'kulaks'. In tsarist Russia the kulak was a peasant with a lot of land who needed to hire farmhands at harvest time, and was generally perceived as a rapacious profiteer. The October Revolution had done away with this sort. But there were still peasants who by dint of luck and/or hard work had become comparatively prosperous during the 1920s. They were least likely to favour collectivisation, and could easily be demonised as small-scale exploiters of the poorer peasants.

ABOVE: Women were brought into the workforce in large numbers during the Five Year Plan. This Muscovite is helping repair a road.

LEFT: A suburban Moscow street in 1934 still has an unpaved road and not a car in sight.

ABOVE RIGHT: Moscow in the 1920s, compared with European capitals such as Berlin, Rome or Paris, was undeveloped.

Kulaks were to suffer endless misery and degradation. Their smallholdings were swallowed up by the state and 5 million of them were deported as forced labour to the bleak northern forests where they died in droves. Along with them went many others who were not kulaks but who opposed Stalin or had found the courage to speak out against collectivisation. One observer at the time noted: 'The best and hardest workers of the land are being taken away, with the misfits and the lazybones staying behind.'

Stalin was rightly concerned about the backwards state of agriculture, with peasants reliant on horse and harrow rather than on the new machinery available to ease their burden and improve output. But his methods of enforcement were barbaric and he showed little remorse for the havoc that he was wreaking. As he justified his policy, he branded kulaks 'the sworn enemies of collectivisation'. He announced 'Our policy is a class policy. He who thinks that one can conduct in the countryside a policy which will please everyone, the rich as well as the poor, is not a Marxist but an idiot, because, comrades, such a policy does not exist in the natural order of things.'

The language Stalin used was as evil as any denunciation of the Jews by Hitler: 'To take the offensive against the kulaks means...to deal the kulak class such a blow that it will no longer rise to its feet....Of course [the kulak] can't be admitted to a collective farm. He can't be because he's an accursed enemy...'

The remaining peasants were often far from keen on the prospects of joining a collective. Before the moment came, they slaughtered their stock and gorged themselves, fearful in the belief that they would get nothing on a collective farm. They saw themselves losing everything and gaining nothing. In 1930 almost a quarter of Russia's peasants were forced into collectives. Six years later 90 per cent of the peasant population had been 'collectivised'. The complexion of the entire countryside was changed beyond recognition and at unprecedented speed. Stalin refused to pace the changes. 'To slow down the tempo would mean falling behind,' he said. 'And those who fall behind get beaten.'

The famine that loomed in the towns and cities during 1928 returned to haunt the countryside in the early 1930s. Rural chaos reigned, with few crops being sown and all the produce being dispatched away as soon as it was ready. Stories abounded of mothers killing and eating their children, of a trade in human flesh for food. The hungry and the desperate ground bones and leather to make flour and scavenged in the undergrowth for insects and small mammals. Perhaps the full horrors will never be known.

Lev Kopelev was one of the eager young Communists who requisitioned food from distraught peasants

LEFT: Lazar Kaganovich (left) and Nikita Khruschev (right) visit a construction site of the Moscow Metro.

RIGHT: The Georgian artist, I M Toidze, commemorated Stalin's visit in 1931 to a hydroelectric project in the Caucasus with this painting. It pointed the way to the cult of the personality that was to dominate Soviet culture in the postwar years.

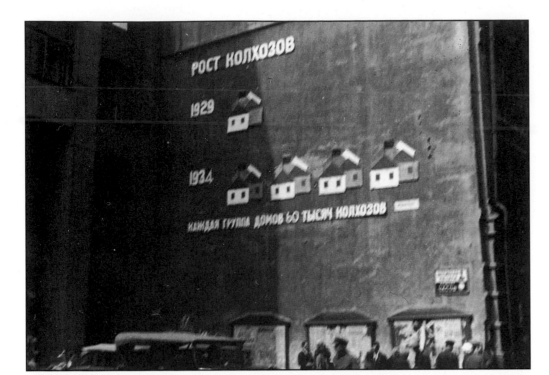

LEFT: Soviet citizens took pride in the achievements of their industry, which were put on public display whenever possible. These statistics boast of housing construction in Moscow.

BELOW: Stalin used the Soviet propaganda machine to identify himself with heroic workers such as these cotton growers.

and their hungry families. His fanatical ideology is evidenced by the following chilling statement: 'Our great goal was the universal triumph of Communism, and for the sake of that goal, everything was permissible – to lie, to steal, to destroy hundreds of thousands and even millions of people.'

As food was shipped out of the countryside to the towns, the hungry peasants were tempted to hoard or to sabotage the transport which was taking away their salvation. In response, Stalin ordered trials, with children accusing their parents of crimes against the state. By 1932 Stalin had forbidden collective farmers from leaving their villages.

Collectivisation had produced some statistical success. State purchase of grain doubled between 1928 and 1931 while exports soared. For Stalin had to send the majority of food produced in the USSR abroad in

RIGHT: The first two Five Year Plans swept away old Russian cities and replaced churches and narrow streets with modern office blocks and broad avenues. The State Trade commission was built during the early 1930s.

BELOW: 'We are advancing full steam ahead – to socialism, leaving behind the age-old "Russian" backwardness.' – J. Stalin, *Pravda*, 1929

LEFT: In January 1934 Stalin opened the 17th Party Congress, the so-called Congress of Victors, and celebrated the triumph of the First Five Year Plan. Yet of the 1966 delegates who attended, 1108 would be arrested during the purges that followed.

BOTTOM LEFT: This certificate was awarded to an activist who eliminated kulaks in Uzbekistan. The recipient received a silk gown.

TOP RIGHT: This Moscow block of flats was erected during the first Five Year Plan.

BOTTOM RIGHT: The bounteous table of this Ukrainian collective farm stands as a testament to the success of the collectivisation of agriculture.

order to find the money to pay for the industrial technology needed for an ambitious factory-building programme – even though the bodies of the starving littered the streets. However, the peak soon passed. By 1935, production had slumped. The lesson that an unhappy workforce did not work well appeared lost on Stalin, who later admitted that as many as 10 million had perished. Yet his attitude towards death was bizarre. 'One death is a tragedy,' he would say. 'A million just statistics.'

THE GREAT TERROR

BY 1934 Stalin held sway over the Soviet Union as party general secretary. Although his power was not absolute, he had ensured that key jobs were held by his supporters. However, there was a politburo which could overrule him and candidates sufficiently popular to take his place. Stalin decided to make his position unassailable with one of the bloodiest episodes of modern times, the Great Purge.

It was sparked by the death of Sergei Kirov, secretary to the central committee and party boss in Leningrad. His assassin was a disgruntled Communist called Leonid Nikolayev who lurked in the toilets of the Smolny Institute in Leningrad before leaping out and shooting Kirov in the back of the neck.

While Kirov had once been a close associate of Stalin's, the gulf between the two had been growing. Kirov had been championing the cause of the workers and had demanded that Stalin improved conditions both in industry and agriculture. Kirov was also being proposed as an alternative general secretary by those in the party left unconvinced by Stalin's brand of communism. Opposition to Stalin emerged in the form of a seven-page document in 1932, which indicted Stalin with a betrayal of Leninism. The so-called Riutin Appeal called for the removal of Stalin from the leadership and the release of Trotskyites from prison. Stalin wanted Comrade Riutin and his cohorts shot but the politburo refused to allow it. Instead Riutin was imprisoned and the so-called Riutin counter-revolutionary group – which included Zinoviev and Kamenev – was expelled from the party.

So the shooting of Kirov gave Stalin a lever to use against his still-active opponents. He may even have organised it himself. The instant consequence was that scores of people were accused of the crime – anyone

LEFT: As Stalin's personality cult developed, he was identified with heroic airmen – Stalin's falcons – such as Valery Chkalov, shown here with the Soviet leader after his flight from Udd Island in the Arctic Circle. This stunt was timed to precede the 1936 show trial, giving an example of Soviet heroism to contrast with the Trotskyite-Zinovievite 'traitors'.

RIGHT: Sergei Kirov succeeded Zinoviev as Leningrad party boss. In January 1934 he was extremely popular in the party, and was elected secretary of the Central Committee. His assassination in December 1934 triggered the Great Terror.

LEFT: Georgi Piatakov was an Old Bolshevik ally of Trotsky who survived Trotsky's downfall to become an important administrator of heavy industrial projects during the Five Year Plan. He was put on trial in January 1937 and executed.

TOP RIGHT: Stalin waves to the masses with Sergo Ordzhonikidze (right) and Kliment Voroshilov (left) from the Lenin mausoleum.

BOTTOM RIGHT: Genrikh Iagoda (second from left) was in charge of the NKVD during the earliest stages of the Terror. He had been associated with the Soviet police since its earliest days. But he was not a Stalinist, and his attempt to protect his political allies Nikolai Bukharin and Aleksei Rykov from Stalin's clutches cost him his job and his life.

whose names appeared in the files of the secret police being arrested and interrogated. The charges were then expanded to cover those considered enemies of the Soviet Union. Thousands were deported to the Gulag where they would perish.

Then the show trials began. The first was held in January 1935 and it was repeated in August 1936. In the dock on both occasions were Zinoviev and Kamenev, respected Old Bolsheviks who had once shared power with Stalin. They had been the target of Stalin's venom for years. Evidence against the defendants was virtually nonexistent, with confessions clearly having been wrung out of them, but that did not stop Prosecutor-General Andrei Vyshinskii branding them 'mad dogs of capitalism'.

The two were sentenced to death and executed almost immediately. Such was the thrall of Stalin that in their last words in court they urged the people to follow their leader.

In the following two years there was a frenzy of death, denunciation and paranoia among the population. The Gulag was bursting at the seams, with an estimated population of 8 million. Mass graves were required to cope with the number of bodies.

A succession of public trials revealed that virtually the whole of the Old Bolshevik leadership had at some time or another plotted the downfall of the Soviet Union and the assassination of Comrade Stalin. In January 1937 a group associated with Trotsky were tried and most found guilty. One of the guilty, Georgi Piatakov, was a close associate of Stalin's supporter Sergo Ordzhonikidze. Ordzhonikidze committed suicide shortly after Piatakov's guilt was established. In June 1937 a secret trial wiped out a substantial part of the Red

LEFT: Nikolai Ezhov succeeded Iagoda as NKVD chief in September 1936. He had a reputation as a puritanical anti-bureaucrat and frequently tried to evoke the image of a dedicated Civil-War-era revolutionary in his public appearances. Under Ezhov the Terror reached its height. He disappeared from public view in January 1939, and was shot in secret in 1940.

RIGHT: The great Russian writer Maksim Gorki died in 1936, and his funeral was a public event. But allegations have been made that he was medically murdered on Stalin's orders.

LEFT: The public face of the purges was Andrei Vyshinsky, the chief state prosecutor during the show trials.

TOP RIGHT: Looking at this meeting of the Presidium of the Supreme Soviet of the USSR, one might think that constitutional politics carried on during the 1930s. But the reality was a state where political or administrative failures were punished by trumped-up charges leading to the death penalty

BOTTOM RIGHT: This political agitator is explaining a new system of electing People's Courts to timber workers. A new constitution was promulgated in the USSR in November 1936, guaranteeing all manner of rights to citizens. Someone, somewhere, had a very black sense of humour.

Army's high command, including its best military brain and friend of Kirov, Marshal Mikhail Tukhachevsky. Now the Soviet Union had entered the *Ezhovschina* (Ezhov's time) named for the puritanical NKVD chief Nikolai Ezhov, when the purges were at their height and hundreds of thousands perished.

Ezhov's men pursued their task with relish. Possessing unseemly enthusiasm, they burst into the homes of sleeping families and hauled off innocent victims for torture, beatings, internal exile or execution. There

LEFT: Vyacheslav Molotov speaks to the Supreme Soviet. Molotov, Stalin's deputy, was shrewd enough to know how to flatter the Boss and keep his place.

BELOW: Two Muscovites search for relatives among the victims of Stalinism following Gorbachev's February 1988 speech. The best figures reveal that between 1930 and 1953, 786,098 people out of 3,778,234 sentenced for counter-revolutionary crimes were shot.

is evidence that the NKVD worked on a quota system, killing to fulfil a body count. Anyone and everyone was suspected of 'counter-revolutionary' activity. Minds twisted by Stalinism applied this to all manner of incidents. A faithful belief in Stalin and devotion to the motherland was not sufficient to prevent death. The last great show trial was held in March 1938, when Bukharin and Aleksei Rykov, the so-called Right Deviationists, were found guilty. Finally, the NKVD reaped its grim reward and was itself purged in 1939. Ezhov was replaced by Lavrenti Beria, a slimy Georgian who seems to have taken an abiding personal interest in the art of torture.

The only Old Bolsheviks left were Stalinists – Molotov, Kaganovich, Mikoyan, Voroshilov – or men who had never sought to pursue an independent political line – Kalinin and Petrovsky. Now no one would dare challenge Stalin's authority. A final body count for this 'revolution from above' will never be known.

FAMILY MAN

When Joseph Stalin married for the first time, the bride was chosen by his mother. Yekaterina Svanidze was not interested in politics yet she agreed to wed Stalin who was brash, uncouth and committed to revolutionary socialism. The wedding took place either while he was in jail in 1903 – marriage services behind bars were not rare – or in church in accordance with his mother's wishes while he was in exile. Little is know of their life together, which was tragically short.

She gave birth to their son Yakov in 1908. When the baby was just two months old she died of typhoid fever. As he stood by her coffin, Stalin uttered to a friend: 'This creature softened my stony heart. When she died all warm feeling for people died with her. It is all so desolate here inside, so inexpressibly empty.'

He was to marry again, possibly because he felt a man of his station needed a wife for appearance's sake. He was attracted to the teenage daughter of a revolutionary comrade Sergei Alliluyev. Aged 39, Stalin had already slept with Sergei's wife. Now he set a lustful gaze towards 17-year-old Nadezhda Sergeevna, known as Nadya.

Soon after they married, Nadya bore him a son, Vasily. Two years later they had a daughter, Svetlana. But Nadya had difficulty in adapting to life as a wife and mother. Her family were all revolutionaries and women were treated as equals to men. Stalin felt differently. The role he had in mind for his wife was a submissive one. Nadya could not and would not conform.

BELOW: The leading Russian writer of the day, Maksim Gorki, became a friend of Stalin's family after he made Moscow his summer home in 1931.

To escape the closeted drudgery of life in the Kremlin, Nadya became an aide to Lenin. He trusted her implicitly and gave her the most secret of his documents. Her loyalty to him and the party far outweighed her burden of duty to her husband. Stalin was regularly outraged when she refused to share these secrets with her. After Lenin's death, Nadya moved to the editorial staff of a magazine called Revolution and Culture, once again revelling in her independence.

At home, the children were being brought up by nannies. The household was run by a housekeeper, the cook and the guards from the secret police. Stalin was increasingly involved in the bureaucracy of power. He drank heavily while Nadya, who was affected badly by alcohol, did not drink at all. They slept in separate rooms: she in a finely appointed bedroom with plush rugs and Chanel scent bottles dotting the dressing table, he in a study, next to the governmental red telephone.

Nadya was offered all the privileges that Kremlin women enjoyed. She did not have to worry about how she was going to feed and clothe her family or even who was going to look after them. Nevertheless, she was a passionate socialist and her unease about the conditions of the peasants and workers was growing.

There were bitter rows between Stalin and Nadya. She had run away from him once in 1926 hoping to start a new life but he had summoned her back. In her heart she knew that there was no chance of an escape. She was also prone to depression. For days she would sink into a blackness where she could not be reached. During the frequent blazing rows she had with Stalin he would accuse her of being schizophrenic. She in turn would call him paranoid.

By way of escape, she threw herself into work. She began to study at the Industrial Academy and aimed to become an engineer. But Stalin still overshadowed her existence, as fellow students were persecuted and sent to Gulag (the labour camps). Old comrades, people she had known and trusted all her life, were being branded enemies of the state. Her discomfort at the direction of the regime with her husband at the helm grew ever greater. Yet she was powerless to intervene.

Nadya sought solace in religion, one of the few overt ways that she exploited her position as wife to Stalin. While worship was banned by Stalin's regime, and churches desecrated, Nadya was able to pursue her religious beliefs in relative peace.

By the time of the fifteenth anniversary of the revolution on 7 November 1932, the pressure on Nadya was intense. All who saw her at the celebration parade remarked on her aged face, its grey-white colour and lifeless eyes. That night there was a party for Kremlin bigwigs. Stalin was as coarse and bullying as ever. In his drunkenness he was irritated by his wife's empty glass. 'Oi you, drink,' he bellowed.

'Don't talk to me like that,' screamed Nadya. She stormed out of the party, pursued by Polina Molotova, wife of Prime Minister Vyacheslav Molotov and later to become Stalin's mistress. Polina did her best to soothe Nadya who complained long and hard about Stalin's behaviour. They parted only when Nadya appeared calm once more. As they bade *each other goodnight, Polina never guessed she would be the last person to see Nadya alive.*

Among Nadya's possessions was a small pistol bought for her by her beloved brother Pavel. The next morning Nadya's cold body was found by the housekeeper lying in a pool of blood. Stalin was asleep nearby, recovering from his stupor of the night before. Instead of waking him, the housekeeper called an old friend of Nadya's family and Poina Molotova. It was their grief-stricken wails that finally awoke the dictator.

Her death, according to the newspapers, was due to appendicitis. Her daughter Svetlana who was six at the time, was never told the gory truth and only discovered by chance in reading a magazine in London at the age of 15. Rumour flew around Moscow, however. Stalin was said to have murdered his wife after discovering an affair between her and his son Yakov. Suicide was impossible, declared the gossips, the fatal bullet having penetrated her left temple when she was right-handed. Reports on the death were destroyed, so it is impossible to verify the cause today. However, given her state of mind, it is likely that Nadya did indeed take her own life. Stalin was not only bereft but furious too. 'She went away as an enemy,' he told his friends and stayed away from the funeral.

BELOW: The avuncular image of pipe-smoking Iosif Vissarionovich sits oddly with the reality of a man who could count five suicide attempts among his family and political associates.

WAR LEADER

BEFORE the outbreak of the Second World War, Britain and France had been courting Stalin. As war with Nazi Germany loomed, both governments saw the need to forget past differences and enlist the support of the Soviet tyrant. Hitler apparently had other ideas; the *Führer* had made no secret of his loathing of Communism as an ideal and the Russian people as subhuman Slavs.

Yet in August 1939 Hitler performed a staggering diplomtic U-turn. Out of the blue a non-aggression treaty was signed at the Kremlin by Joachim von Ribbentrop for Germany and Vyacheslav Molotov for the Soviet Union. Stalin met with the German foreign minister afterwards, and Ribbentrop told a joke that he said was doing the rounds in Berlin: 'Stalin will yet join the anti-Comintern pact.'

On the face of it, there were admirable, mutual benefits. Germany would receive grain and oil in exchange for technology. Each promised not to attack the other. However, the real reason for the agreement, a secret protocol that went unpublished until after Germany's surrender in 1945, was masked by those pledges of cordiality. Within two weeks, Hitler and his troops had marched into Poland. The Poles were soon crushed in a lightning war and their country was carved up, with Germany occupying the west and the Red Army moving into the east.

The subjugation of Poland was the most tangible 'benefit' from the pact that Stalin had sought. It gave him a taste for expansion. He looked towards neighbouring Finland. In November 1939 he demanded territory from the tiny country. When its government refused, the Red Army marched in.

But if Stalin was hoping for a German-style blitzkrieg, he was sorely disappointed. Finland was the 'mouse that roared'. Within six weeks, the country's gallant fighters had wreaked havoc with the enemy forces. It was not until March 1940 that Finland was finally brought to heel – by which time more than 150,000 Red Army soldiers had lost their lives. This small country had humiliated its giant neighbour, to Stalin's immense chagrin.

LEFT: Churchill and Stalin pass a guard of honour during the British premier's visit to Moscow in 1944.

RIGHT: Muscovite men gather to get their mobilisation orders on 23 June 1941, two days after the German invasion had begun.

LEFT: Stalin's demands for a Second Front and aid from the Allies brought him into contact with such notorious capitalists as Lord Beaverbrook.

RIGHT: The rains and mud of the Eastern Front in both spring and autumn was a serious hindrance to both sides.

There was no one to blame for the poor performance of the army than Stalin himself. The purge had relieved the Red Army of its finest leaders. By the end of 1938, three out of every five Red Army marshals were dead, as well as 13 out of 15 army commanders. More than half of the country's divisional commanders had lost their lives. The Red Army, the largest in the world, suffered from an acute shortage of direction and know-how. Those left to assume command were generally the worst and weakest.

Hitler watched with interest the failings of the Red Army in action. The ill-conceived war against Finland confirmed his belief that the 'Russian bear' could be beaten. The Führer's hidden agenda – of war against Stalin, the Soviet Union and its people – came to the fore.

The spring of 1941 brought a distraction for Hitler in the Balkans when his forces attacked Greece and Yugoslavia. Victory was quick and Hitler turned his attentions to the Soviet Union. It was a late spring, and Russia's primitive roads were left clogged by mud during the slow thaw. So it was June before an attack against Russia was deemed appropriate.

On the morning of 22 June 1941, the last delivery of grain under the Hitler-Stalin pact chugged out of the Soviet Union by train… as German soldiers poured in. Operation Barbarossa, the code-name for the attack on the Soviet Union, involved 2.5 million men in 165 German divisions. The assault came in three prongs, one headed for Kiev, the next for Leningrad and a third for Moscow.

Russian commanders were flummoxed. Orders to defend their homeland were given belatedly by Stalin (See 'Stalin's Greatest Blunder' on page 75) who for 11 days did nothing as the Red Army fell back in disarray. The Soviet leader was only stung into action when it became clear that many of his people were not resisting the Nazis but welcoming them as liberators.

In communities along the front, long-silent church bells rang out – not to warn against but to welcome the invaders. In the newly occupied towns, Christians, for years refused the right to worship, joyfully

LEFT: Women and elderly men dig anti-tank trenches during the autumn of 1941.

RIGHT: A propaganda poster urges Soviet citizens to defend the Motherland against the Nazis.

assembled in churches for services. Many civilians, especially peasant farmers, welcomed what seemed to be an end to the purges and the beginnings of the freedoms promised in 1917. Even the Jews, victims of Stalin's anti-Semitism, responded willingly to Nazi posters asking them to register with the invaders.

As Hitler predicted, the Red Army was no match for the skill of the German. Stalin at first disappeared from public view, but after 3 July 1941 he exerted total control over Soviet strategy. His reply to the German onslaught was to order his men to launch ill-advised, ill-organised counterattacks. Those who retreated were considered cowards and shot. However, the situation as the Red Army recoiled from the frontiers was so confused, that it is unlikely that Stalin could have altered events even if he had been history's greatest military genius. The prospects for the Red Army's soldiers were grim.

Disillusioned troops, assured by their leaders that invasion was impossible, surrendered by the myriad. In four months, the conquering army of just over 3 million were to capture almost over 2.5 million of the Red Army. In German hands, the prisoners were treated with contempt, deprived of food, clothes and adequate shelter. Thousands were sent back to Germany to almost certain death in the Nazi labour camps.

Hitler was dazzled by the success of his conquering forces. 'Russia will be finished in three weeks', his generals told him. The only blot on his horizon was the way the motorised panzer divisions had outstripped the infantry. Following two months of hectic advances, Hitler chose to redirect his main thrust. He ordered several armies to veer away from Moscow to Kiev. The generals were astonished and horrified. Even after Kiev had fallen, Moscow and Leningrad remained still some distance away from the leading German units.

LEFT: Red Army soldiers on their way to the front march through Leningrad under the eyes of a statue of Kirov.

RIGHT: German prisoners captured in Stalingrad are marched away to camps.

Hitler's generals were rightly concerned about the risks of being entrenched outside the cities during the harsh Russian winter. Before long the first autumn rains came, to be followed by the first chill of winter. Residents of both cities made good use of the unexpected respite. As the Germans fumed in abeyance, the Russians fortified their cities with anti-tank ditches, barbed-wire walls and earthworks.

The resumed German advance was slowed by boggy roads, broken machinery and weary men and horses. At the gates of Moscow the German army was brought to a standstill. Happily, although the enemy was in the western suburbs, Muscovites were still receiving supplies from the east. In Leningrad there was a siege which was to last for 900 days. In the encircled city 2 million citizens died from starvation, privation and disease before the cordon was lifted.

The winter weather came to the rescue of Russia, just as it had in 1812 when Napoleon's forces were defeated. German soldiers experienced the miseries of freezing months spent in the open. Hundreds were killed by enemy action during the winter deadlock but many thousands more fell victim to frostbite.

Also to the Soviet Union's advantage was the enormous volume of manpower available to fight for the

Motherland. So while the casualty rate was enormous, there were still more soldiers coming forward to man the front lines. The German chiefs of staff declared: 'We estimated that we should have to contend with 180 Russian divisions; we have already counted 360.'

The third trump was the productivity of Soviet industry which, through patriotic fervour and an astonishing rebirth of effort, kept its men at war supplied with arms and machines, outstripping the manufacture of German goods.

In the factories, on the farms and cities and on the front line, it would be a long and arduous grind to victory for the people of the Soviet Union. Hitler sent in special task forces called *Einsatzgruppen* which massacred Jews, Communists, gypsies and other so-called undesirables en route through Russia. Civilians who escaped ill-treatment from the Germans had their own countrymen to fear. The NKVD slaughtered scores in the prisons of towns like Lvov before they fell to the Germans.

As the Red Army became more effective under the leadership of outstanding generals like Georgi Zhukov, so the balance of the war changed. A failed Soviet offensive in the spring of 1942, was followed by a major German offensive in the south aiming to seize the oil fields of the Caucasus that culminated in the fierce battle for Stalingrad – perhaps the Red Army's greatest victory.

The Germans in spring 1943 attacked around the town of Kursk, fought the largest tank battle in history, and were badly beaten by a well-prepared enemy. A push by the Red Army launched on the third anniversary of the invasion brought its troops back to the Polish border in August 1944. For the first time in the war, the conflict was being carried into the Third Reich's territory. As a bonus, thousands of German troops had been tied up on the Eastern Front, enabling the Allies to execute the D-Day landings on the beaches of Normandy and to begin the liberation of Western Europe.

LEFT: A T-34 tank is repaired in the tractor factory during the fighting for Stalingrad.

TOP RIGHT: Averill Harriman (on right), the US ambassador to the Soviet Union, presents scrolls of honour from President Roosevelt to the cities of Leningrad and Stalingrad.

RIGHT: Georgi Zhukov was the best Red Army commander of the war.

FAR RIGHT: Kliment Voroshilov was Stalin's military sidekick from the days of the Civil War. His understanding of modern combined arms' warfare left something to be desired.

In January 1945 Russian forces freed the 800 sickly prisoners abandoned at Auschwitz, the notorious concentration camp. Author Primo Levi, who was one of them, described their reaction to the human corpses which met them: 'They did not greet us nor did they smile; they seemed oppressed not only by compassion but by a confused restraint which sealed their lips and bound their eyes to the funereal scene. It was that shame we knew so well; the shame the Germans did not know; the feeling of guilt that such a crime should exist...'

LEFT: Members of the 1st Minsk Partisan Brigade receive an award for gallantry in 1944.

TOP RIGHT: A Red Army nurse struggles to help a wounded comrade to safety.

BOTTOM RIGHT: The German commanders defending Berlin sign their surrender.

LEFT: After the Red Army's victory over Germany, a sizable part of it was sent to Siberia, where it attacked the huge Japanese army garrisoning Manchuria. The Japanese were beaten, and here some of their soldiers surrender their weapons.

Three months later and the Russian forces fought their way house by street to the Reichstag in Berlin.

The toll of the Second World War on the Soviet people was 20 million, a loss far greater than any other nation. Yet Stalin was the acclaimed hero of the hour. He accepted the title of 'Generalissimus'. At summit conferences of the war leaders, he rubbed shoulders with Churchill and US President Franklin D Roosevelt, international heavyweights who were poles apart from him ideologically but united in their aim of smashing Hitler. Together the trio planned a new world order to follow the ending of hostilities. Stalin revelled in his new image of wise elder statesman. Sadly, the ties that bound the three nations together in times of strife were not strong enough to survive the ravages of peace.

STALIN'S GREATEST BLUNDER

If the greatest mistake in the whole of the Second World War was Hitler's attack on the Soviet Union, then the second greatest mistake was Stalin's reaction to it. Or, rather, lack of reaction. At the end of the conflict, when the analyses of the conduct of the war were made and the reckoning taken, it was Stalin's personal handling of his greatest crisis that was the most discreditable. History is not favourable to the Georgian bully.

In spring 1941, as German forces mustered on the Soviet Union's southerly borders, dire warnings had been dispatched to Stalin of the impending attack. Historians have noted that as many as 76 different alerts were sent to Moscow. Britain's prime minister, Winston Churchill, was happy to bury the differences of the past in order to prepare Stalin. Spies from across the world sent back the alarming news. One German soldier, a committed Communist, even deserted to bring word of Hitler's intentions to Stalin well in time for his forces to react.

However, nothing could persuade stubborn Stalin that his ally Germany would break its pact. If attack was going to come, he felt certain it would be from Japan. Such was his faith in Hitler that he ordered his commanders not to fortify the border. Stalin even had the runaway German soldier shot.

BELOW: Molotov stood in for Stalin as the public face of the regime during the war's first days.

Stalin was lucky to have a military genius heading his armies. He was the chief of staff, General Georgi Zhukov, who on the afternoon of 21 June – the eve of war – was sufficiently confident in his border intelligence units to hand his leader a piece of paper bearing the draft of a directive to the Soviet armed forces placing them on maximum alert. Stalin handed it back, saying gruffly: 'This order is premature. Draw up another to the effect that on the night of June 21-22 there may be provocation on the border. The troops must be ready for it but they must not be incited by any provocations which might lead to complications'.

Zhukov scurried away to redraft the warning. The final, approved version was not in fact issued until the early hours of Sunday 22 June and were not read by many front-line commanders until they were actually under shellfire! Only one element of the armed forces, the navy, had by that time been mobilised for war – and then only on its own initiative. In the end, it was the navy that first alerted the Kremlin to the fact that the country was being invaded.

At 3.15 a.m. the commander of the Black Sea Fleet telephoned the Kremlin with the news that the Luftwaffe was bombing the Sevastopol naval base. The call was taken by Admiral Nikolai Kuznetsov, the duty naval commissar at the Kremlin, who, prepared for the crisis, had set up a

LEFT: Stalin did not speak to the peoples of the Soviet Union until 3 July 1941, 13 days after the Germans had attacked.

RIGHT: Churchill presents the Stalingrad Sword in honour of the greatest Red Army victory of the war. The image of Stalin as a strategic genius was already being promoted through propaganda, regardless of his conduct at the war's beginning.

Все наши силы—на поддержку нашей героической Красной Армии, нашего славного Красного Флота!

Все силы народа—на разгром врага!

Вперед, за нашу победу!

Выступление по радио Государственного Комитета Обороны И. В. СТАЛИНА.

3 июля 1941 года.

camp bed in his office. The admiral immediately tried to contact Stalin's office. When Admiral Kuznetsov finally got through, the duty officer told him: 'He's not here and I don't know where he is.'

In fact, the Soviet leader had been driven to his villa outside the city and had gone to bed. and had left orders not to be disturbed.

It was probably at around 4.30 a.m. – the very moment that the entire might of the Nazi military machine was being thrown against the unprepared Russian armies across the entire front, that Zhukov himself finally telephoned Stalin's villa. The phone rang and rang until eventually the sleepy voice of an officer answered. In response to the Chief of Staff's urgent summons, the man could only blurt out: 'Comrade Stalin is asleep.'

Zhukov commanded: 'Wake him up immediately. The Germans are bombing our cities.'

It was several minutes more before Stalin picked up the phone. When Zhukov outlined the scale of the catastrophe, Stalin fell silent. 'Do you understand me?' Zhukov pleaded. His leader answered by calling a meeting of the Politburo.

By the time the political leadership had been hastily assembled, the

spring sunshine was filtering through the trees of the Moscow parks.
Stalin stunned his audience by asking: 'Don't you think all this might be
a provocation?' Even at 7.15 p.m., with his border defences blasted apart
in a hundred places, Stalin was still clinging to the hope that this was not
a 'real attack' and seeking 'clarification of the position' from his envoys
in Berlin. He ordered that the Red Army repel the invaders but not
retaliate by entering German occupied territory.

Hours later, he realised that he had been duped by a greater dictator.
Staring into space, devoid of emotion as well as action, he said simply:
'All that Lenin created we have lost forever.' Then he ordered his car
and retreated to his villa – not to be seen for 10 days.

Sunday 22 June 1941 was a fine day in Moscow. Families promenaded
in the warmth. At 11.30 a.m.the loudspeakers in the main streets, which
traditionally played marches and light music, suddenly a voice broke in.

'Vnimaniye! Vnimaniye!' (Attention! Attention!)

The Muscovites listened in anticipation as an announcer told them
that there was to be important broadcast at noon. The music did not
return. Instead a metronome began ticking.

At noon, as promised, the metronome stopped. Then the Foreign
Minister, Vyacheslav Molotov, spoke:

    Men and women, citizens of the Soviet Union, the Soviet
government and its head, Comrade Stalin, have instructed me to

BELOW: Joseph Stalin arriving at the Livadia Palace where the Yalta conference was held.

ABOVE: By the end of the war, Stalin's military skill had markedly improved. Indeed, of the Big Three, he was probably the one who understood modern warfare best.

make the following announcement. At 4 a.m., without declaration of war and without any claims being made on the Soviet Union, German troops attacked our country, attacked our frontier in many places and bombed from the air Zhitomir, Kiev, Sevastopol, Kaunus and other cities. The attack has been made despite the fact that there was a non-aggression pact between the Soviet Union and Germany, a pact the terms of which were scrupulously observed by the Soviet Union. Our cause is just. The enemy will be crushed. Victory will be ours.

The was a moment's stunned silence, then pandemonium. Over the next few hours, fearful Muscovites swept through the city's food stores, stocking up for the siege of their country that they knew was coming. If they ever wondered why Molotov had made the dramatic announcement rather than Stalin, they probably assumed that their leader was busying himself with the war effort. They could not have been wrong. Joseph Stalin sat in his villa in a state of near paralysis.

THE NEW TSAR

AT the end of the war, Germany and its capital Berlin were divided into four sectors. They fell under the control of the victorious nations Britain, the United States, France and the Soviet Union. Even before the war was finished, the Allies had agreed to seek reparations from Germany and each zone was to provide compensation for its occupying country. Stalin took full advantage of the agreement. Complete factories were dismantled and transported to the USSR, along with key workers. Stalin was determined to wring as much as possible out of the vanquished Germany, to the consternation of the rest of the Allies.

Stalin had been courteous toward Churchill and Roosevelt and held them in high regard. But before the end of the war Churchill had been replaced as British premier by Clement Atlee in a general election and Roosevelt had died. His successor Harry Truman was less accommodating towards Stalin. Although Britain, America and France had during wartime paved the way for the unforeseen Communist domination of eastern Europe, the victorious countries were now unhappy about the arrangement.

For his part, Stalin became increasingly suspicious; his prewar paranoia had returned. He was convinced that the western Allies had dragged their feet in the conflict so that Germany and the USSR fought each other for as long as possible in the hope that both would be destroyed. He threw a cloak of secrecy over eastern Europe.

LEFT: Andrei Zhdanov took on the mantle of cultural commissar in the postwar Soviet Union. He was not well remembered by artists after his death in 1948.

RIGHT: This crystal globe, from the workers of the glass industry of Poland, was presented to Stalin in 1947.

LEFT: 43 Mayakovsky Square in Moscow was a typical example of the kind of architectural style favoured in Stalin's empire. Buildings resembling this one were erected throughout the capitals of eastern Europe, symbols of Stalin's dominance.

RIGHT: This frieze in a Moscow Metro station is typical of the postwar personality cult. It was almost as if the 70-years-old man was trying to use it to defy his approaching death.

On a visit to the USA in 1946, Winston Churchill spoke prophetically about the seriously deteriorating relations with Stalin: 'Nobody knows what Soviet Russia and its Communist International [abolished in 1943] organisation intends to do in the immediate future or what are the limits, if any, of their expansive and proselytising tendencies. From Stettin on the Baltic to Trieste on the Adriatic, an iron curtain has descended across the continent.'

Stalin, even in the 1920s, expressed a preference for the Soviet Union's immediate neighbours to be countries with Communist regimes. Gradually, Communist governments took power in the countries of Eastern Europe – Poland and Rumania in 1947, Bulgaria, Czechoslovakia and Hungary in 1948. The Soviet troops who had liberated these countries from Nazism now in their turn became oppressors. People who had fled before the arrival of the Soviet troops were handed back to face unknown horrors. Red Army soldiers who had been prisoners of war in German territories were likewise transported home. In Stalin's eyes they were guilty of cowardice and betrayal. Many were executed without trial, the remainder were mostly worked to death.

Worse was to come. A US aid plan devised by Secretary of State George Marshall in 1948 assisted the ruined economies of western European countries with food, fuel, raw materials and machinery. Stalin viewed it as American expansionism of the worst order. In the same year the western countries decided to unite the divided zones of Germany. The Soviet response was to isolate allied West Berlin in the heart of the

Soviet zone. For a year the western countries airlifted supplies to the sector. Even when the stalemate was broken, West Berlin remained a free port in the midst of the Communist world.

And that world was by now an empire. Added to the Soviet Union at the end of the Second World War were parts of Finland, Rumania and Czechoslovakia, half of Poland and East Prussia, and the Baltic States. And by entering the war against Japan at the last moment, he had 'legitimised' the annexation of the Kurile Islands, Sakhalin Island and parts of Mongolia. His sinister rule now stretched from the Sea of Japan to the River Elbe in Germany. And just as Hitler's propaganda minister, Joseph Goebbels, had predicted in the dying days of Nazi Germany, mass butchery began within those heavily fortified borders.

At home, life for the victorious Soviet peoples was horrific. There was a woeful shortage of housing, severe rationing and Draconian working conditions. There were uprisings among the cold and hungry, each one ruthlessly suppressed. Communist ideals such as collectivisation were once again enforced with a vengeance. The result was a famine in the Ukraine. Party chief of the region Nikita Khrushchev, a future Soviet leader, made a personal plea to Stalin. He received a characteristically brutish reply. 'You're being soft-bellied!' Khrushchev was told. 'They are deceiving you. They are counting on being able to appeal to your sentimentality.'

Gulag was again filled with prisoners as the NKVD relaunched their purges. Whole peoples suspected of having collaborated with the Nazis – Chechens, the Crimean Tartars, Kalmyks and Karachi-Balkars – were transported to starvation in Central Asia and Siberia. Returning soldiers who had witnessed too much of Western life were interrogated and shot.

In Leningrad, the heroic city which had suffered so badly during the war, there was a purge by party chief Andrei Zhdanov against intellectuals, artists and poets. Composers Dmitri Shostakovich and Sergei Prokofiev were under fire for not writing tunes which could be whistled by a worker. Stalin viewed such activities with approval – until he realised that Zhdanov was creating a power base of his own. Although Zhdanov died of natural causes, there followed a purge against the party officials in Leningrad. Unlike the prewar purges, this one did not involve a show trial; those purged were shot out of hand.

Stalin was fearful of intrigue and conspiracy. His daughter Svetlana described her father as being 'as bitter as could be against the whole world. He saw enemies everywhere. It had reached the point of being pathological, of being persecution mania.'

Even in the Kremlin, Stalin wore a bulletproof vest. He travelled in an armour-plated car with bulletproof windows 7cm/2 ¾in thick. His food came from a NKVD farm and was tested by bodyguards for poison before every meal. He did not even like appearing above ground; tunnels were dug to link his office with other government departments, and the Moscow underground was extended to his suburban villa at Kuntsevo. The man had become a prisoner of his own terror.

LEFT: A full table is found in front of this family of collective farm workers, a monument to the success of collectivisation. But at what human cost?

RIGHT: In 1946 Kalinin, the long-standing figurehead executive of the USSR, died. His coffin is carried by the members of the politburo to be buried under the Kremlin wall. He was succeeded by Nikolai Shvernik, Stalin's trade union boss.

In the last few years of his life, Stalin's anti-Semitism reached new heights. He unleashed a tide of retribution against Jews whom he described as 'rootless cosmopolitans'. His addled brain then created another grotesque conspiracy. In January 1953 Moscow Radio announced that Kremlin doctors were plotting to murder the leaders of the country, Stalin included. The unfortunate doctors were branded 'killers in white coats' and were carted off to Moscow's notorious Lubyanka, headquarters of the secret police, for interrogation and certain death. The cauldron of anti-Semitism looked set to boil over.

But on 2 March 1953 Stalin's train of terror stopped in its tracks. On that day the Soviet tyrant suffered a brain haemorrhage and fell into a coma. Over the next few days he was slowly suffocated by a lack of oxygen and his brain was gradually destroyed. His daughter Svetlana, who was at his bedside, later recalled: 'The last hours were nothing but a slow strangulation. The death agony was terrible. He literally choked to death as we watched.'

Stalin died at 9.50 p.m. on 5 March. It was announced the following day to the people of Russia on Moscow Radio: 'The heart of Joseph Vissarionovich Stalin, Lenin's comrade-in-arms and the genius-endowed continuer of his work, has ceased to beat.'

For three days Stalin's body lay in state in the Hall of Columns. Hordes of people filed before it, six abreast. The *New York Times*'s correspondent, Harrison Salisbury, regarded it as a genuine outporing of emotion. Before the doors closed there was a queue some seven miles long. Amid the crush of humanity, countless people died and were trodden underfoot. The troops refused to act until they had instructions.

On 9 March Stalin's coffin was ceremonially taken to the Mausoleum on Red Square and there was a national 10-minutes' silence. Those who mourned him felt he represented stability and order in their vast and disparate nation.

The Soviet Union – or the Union of Soviet Socialist Republics (USSR) to give it its full title – was the world's largest sovereign state. A federation of 15 union republics, with another 20 autonomous republics and several smaller provinces. It occupied an area of 22.5 million sq km/8.65 million sq miles from Iran to the Arctic Circle, from Czechoslovakia to China. It was unwieldy and needed more than the bombast of a bully like Joseph Stalin to hold it together.

LEFT: Nikolai Voznesensky was a close associate of Zhdanov, and highly regarded as a possible successor to Stalin. After Zhdanov's death, secret police chief Lavrenti Beria and his political ally Georgi Malenkov, who sought to succeed Stalin themselves, had Voznesensky arrested and charged him with treason. Stalin was apparently reluctant to sentence the talented Voznesensky, but eventually Beria had his way, thanks to his astute ability to gauge the Boss's moods.

RIGHT: The Soviet Union was a cosmopolitan state. These Kirghizians were one of 104 officially recognised nationalities. The whole structure fell apart rapidly in 1991, once the unifying force of the Communist Party, Stalin's instrument of controlling the masses, was gone.

BURYING STALIN

THE personality cult of Stalinism crumbled astonishingly quickly after his death. He was succeeded as First Secretary of the Communist Party of the Soviet Union and prime minister by Georgi Malenkov. A few days later, Malenkov lost the secretary ship to Nikita Khrushchev. Collective leadership had returned to the Soviet Union.

The NKVD apparatus of fear, which had mushroomed to 1.5 million men and women, was scaled down and renamed the KGB. Its reviled leaders were executed within months of Stalin's death. First to go was Laventi Beria, a contender for leadership, who was arrested at a meeting of the Politburo, unceremoniously hauled into a secret court for a brief trial and shot.

The masses of the USSR, fed information only through the official propaganda machine, were not immediately aware of the dramatic changes at their country's helm. They were not immediately told of the barbaric excesses of the recently lauded Stalin. It was not until 1956, at the 20th Party Congress, that Khrushchev's Secret Speech described in any detail the crimes committed under Stalin's regime and denounced Stalin's 'cult of personality'.

LEFT: The extraordinarily unpleasant Lavrenti Beria, Stalin's last secret police chief, did not long survive his master's death. Despite being Prime Minister Malenkov's ally, he was shot in the summer of 1953.

RIGHT: Lazar Kaganovich was number three in the Stalinist hierarchy before losing his place to Beria after the war. He was eventually purged from the leadership in 1957, after attempting to topple Khrushchev from power. In Stalin's day he would have been shot, but in this kinder, gentler era he was allowed to live on in quiet retirement.

Yet even then this was kept from the mass of Soviet citizenry. It received wider circulation among the foreign Communist parties. As news travelled across world, many were stunned. Their loyalty to avuncular Stalin was beyond question. For years they had blamed the purges on secret police chiefs and the privations on industrial wreckers.

At the 22nd Party Congress in 1961, Stalin's reputation was further tarnished, as the regime he led was accused of 'criminal violations of Socialist legality'. The leadership of the Soviet Union now hauled down his statues. His preserved body was removed from the Lenin Mausoleum and buried by the Kremlin Wall, a demotion to the second rank of the Soviet pantheon.

Yet sadly the turn-about did not herald a new era of freedom. The peoples of the Soviet Union had to wait another 30 years for that…for *glasnost*, for the tearing down of the Iron Curtain and for the final removal of the last vestiges of the tyrannical regime of a Georgian peasant called Joseph Stalin.

LEFT: Anastas Mikoyan supported Khrushchev's anti-Stalinist efforts of the 1950s, in spite of having been a close associate of Stalin.

TOP RIGHT: Stalin was interred in the Lenin Mausoleum, and his name was given equal prominence to the Revolution's mastermind. His body was removed following Khrushchev's speech to the 22nd Party Congress in 1962.

BOTTOM RIGHT: Khrushchev was the most liberal Soviet leader until the days of Gorbachev during the 1980s. However, his attempts to open up the Soviet system led to his downfall.

LEFT: Sculptor Sergei Merkurov's heroic statue of Stalin made the 'Man of Steel' into a 'Man of Marble', but fails to capture how he ruled the Soviet Union from a throne of blood.

PRINCIPAL DATES

1879   Stalin is born on 21 December.

1890   Enters Gori Theological School. Father dies.

1894   Enters Tbilisi Seminary.

1898   Joins Tbilisi Marxists.

1900   Finds work at Tbilisi Observatory.

1901   Loses job and goes underground.

1902   Arrested.

1903   Sentenced to three years' exile in Siberia in July.

1904   Escapes from Siberia in February and marries later that year.

1908   First son Yakov is born on 16 March. Within a month he is arrested and imprisoned and by November he is in exile in Vologda.

1909   Escapes from exile. His first wife dies.

1910   Arrested at Baku and exiled.

1911   Completes exile and moves to St Petersburg, where he is arrested and exiled once more.

1912   Escapes from exile in March and is arrested in St Petersburg two months later and again exiled. He finally escapes in September.

1913   Adopts the name Stalin, meaning 'Man of Steel'. Previously known as Koba, meaning 'the indomitable'. Arrested in St Petersburg and exiled to the Arctic Circle.

1917   Rejected for army service, being medically unfit. Works on Pravda, the Communist Party newspaper during the March revolution. In November he becomes Commissar for Nationalities.

1918   In charge of grain collection in southern Russia. Exacts grain from Tsaritsyn in the face of enemy action.

1919   Declines various posts to stay in Moscow and secure a power base.

1922   Lenin suffers his first stroke in May.

1923   Lenin threatens to break off relations with him in March, shortly before the leader suffers his third stroke.

1924   Lenin dies on 21 January.

1925   Trotsky is removed as Commissar for War.

1928   Trotsky is exiled then expelled from the USSR.

1932   Stalin's second wife, Nadezhda Allilueva, commits suicide.

1934   Kirov is assassinated.

1935   Show trial of Zinoviev, Kamenev and others, followed by another the next year. The terror begins.

1939   Non-Aggression Pact signed between USSR and Germany in August. The Second World War breaks out the following month.

1940   Trotsky is assassinated.

1941   Stalin replaces Molotov as Soviet prime minister in May. 'Operation Barbarossa' brings USSR into the war in June. Stalin appoints himself commander-in-chief of the Red Army.

1942   Red Army holds *Wehrmacht* at bay in Moscow.

1943   Battle of Stalingrad won by Red Army in February. Battle of Kursk won by Red Army in July. Stalin meets Roosevelt and Churchill in Teheran Conference.

1944   900-day Leningrad siege is over. Red Army wins back much of eastern Europe.

1945   Yalta Conference, with Stalin, Churchill and Roosevelt in February. Victory in Europe by May. The map of Europe is redrawn at Potsdam Conference by Stalin, Truman and Atlee. In August Stalin declares war on Japan, less than a month before it surrenders.

1952   Last major public speech made by Stalin at the 19th Congress of the Communist Party of the Soviet Union.

1953   Stalin dies on 5 March.